Donna Kakonge

Old Romance

Donna Kakonge grew up in Toronto and trained as a journalist at Carleton University in Ottawa, Canada from 1990 to 1994. Her first attempt at fiction was a novel she wrote at the age of 17 after reading Danielle Steele and Stephen King, as well as *Sweet Valley High* books. She did not publish this book, later titled *My Roxanne*, until 2007. She has written many freelance articles and reviews for newspapers, magazines and online sources. Her first published short story came out of a creative writing workshop at Carleton University with Tom Henighan and was featured in *Headlight Anthology* – a Concordia University student-published journal. Kakonge did her MA in media studies at Concordia from 1997 to 1999. She has taught at Carleton and Concordia Universities as a teaching assistant. She has also taught a full course at Concordia University and overseas at Makerere University in Kampala, Uganda. From 2006 to the present, Kakonge teaches at Centennial College, Seneca College and

Trebas Institute all in Toronto. She has worked as a journalist on and off with the Canadian Broadcasting Corporation from 1992 to 2007. She received an award from Carleton University as the graduating student with the most promise of becoming an exceptional journalist in honour of the late journalist Marjorie Nichols. The monetary part of the award came from Canadian Senator Pamela Wallin. She has also received a Gemini nomination for a pilot episode of a television show that aired on the Discovery Channel, plus numerous scholarships to attend the

Innoversity Diversity Summit in Toronto. She

has also received a Quebecor Documentary

Fellowship. Kakonge is also the author of

What Happened to the Afro?, *How to Write*

Creative Non-fiction, *Spiderwoman*, *Morning*

English Lessons, *In My Pocket*, editor of *Being*

Healthy: Selected Works from the Internet,

writer of *Do Not Know*, *My Story of*

Transportation, *Draft*: *eSpirituality Chats*,

reporter and producer of a CD of radio

documentaries called "Nine," writer of

Journalism Stories Collection, *Digital Journals*

and Numerology, *Where I Was*, *Draft: Part*

Two, Radio and Television Announcing,

Ugandan Travelogue and narrated two audio

stories from *Spiderwoman*; "Matoke" and

"Church Sunday." The latter appeared in

Headlight Anthology. *School Works* is a

collection of essays written at the

undergraduate and graduate level. *Yes,*

School Works are all communications essays

written while she did graduate work in

Montreal with Concordia University. *School*

Works – Other Essays are from

undergraduate work done at Carleton

University in Ottawa, Canada. *The Best of*

Donna Magazine highlights her online magazine. Old Romance is Kakonge's 32nd book. It is a book of short stories about old romances. Donna Kakonge lives in Toronto, Canada.

www.donnakakonge.com

BOOKS AND CDS BY DONNA KAKONGE

What Happened to the Afro?

How to Write Creative Non-fiction

Spiderwoman

My Roxanne

Being Healthy: Selected Works from the

Internet (edited)

Do Not Know

My Story of Transportation

Draft: eSpirituality Chats

"Nine" (CD)

Journalism Stories Collection

Digital Journals and Numerology

"Matoke" (Audio Download)

"Spiderwoman" (Audio Download)

The Education Generation

In My Pocket

Morning English Lessons

Where I Was

Radio and Television Announcing

Draft: Part Two

My Mind Book

Stories in Red and Yellow: Digging up Work
Done in Yesteryear

The Best of Donna Magazine

Dropouts

Old Romance

Old Romance

Donna Kakonge

Lulu.com

FIRST EDITION LULU INTERNATIONAL

EDITION, December 2009

Library and Archives of Canada Cataloguing in

Publication Data

Kakonge, Donna Kay Cindy

Old Romance
ISBN: 978-1-926734-37-8

Book Design by Dreamstime.com

Manufactured in the United States.

To all the men I've loved before.

Katie and Marc

Katie bumped into her boss as she was leaving the Radio Canada International building in Montreal.

"I'm just going to get my I.D.," she told him pointing to the large Radio-Canada tower on Rene-Levesque.

"Katie," he said looking at the cigarette in her hand. "You have a wonderful voice. Always protect it. You must stop smoking...I used to smoke and my wife kept telling me to quit. One day I just stopped and my wife would even clean around the area by the bed where I kept my cigarettes. Finally, after five years, I threw them out. I knew I was done with them."

Katie had a drag of her cigarette feeling high again. "I will Oliver. One day I will."

She sent a quick smile to Oliver before she ran down the street wearing a designer suit.

She was living in Montreal and a co-announcer on a radio program that aired to sub-Saharan Africa. The morning show had her working afternoons one week when she would report, then nights when she would announce.

She lived off the letters that poured in from Africa and the friendship of her co-announcer Tiffany.

She finally reached the Radio-Canada building and spotted the I.D. desk by the door. She saw a short, dark-haired man come up to her.

"Do you work here?" he asked.

"I work at RCI," Katie said. She was not expecting people in the Radio-Canada building to be so friendly.

"I'm doing an internship with 'Dimanche Magazine,'" he held out his hand.

"My name is Marc."

"Marc," Katie repeated the name slowly. "I'm Katie. I came here to get my I.D."

"Me too," he said flashing a smile that made his green eyes twinkle.

They both moved into the line to get their I.D. Marc let Katie go first even though he came out of the line to speak to her.

"What do you do at RCI?" he asked.

"I'm an announcer,producer," Katie went into an explanation about the program she worked for and by time she was done, she was getting her photograph taken and waiting for Marc.

"Would you like to go out for lunch?" Marc asked Katie.

"I have to go back to work."

"Then for dinner."

Katie looked into this young Quebecois's green eyes. Hers were dark brown, almost black – they matched the politicized significance of her skin.

It was March 23, 2000, and her acceptance of dinner with Marc on St.Catherine in the gay village would change life.

· ·

Katie and Marc went out to dinner later that day to a restaurant walking distance from the Radio-Canada building. Katie had just broken up with a colleague working on the French version of the African show. Marc had just broken up with a long-time girlfriend (who was Haitian) that he had known since high school. Neither of them discussed their past relationships. Katie was in an assertive mood and she did outline in detail what she was looking for in a man.

"I want him to be faithful and devoted to me," she started in quickly, forgetting about her coffee which was rare for her. "I want him to be spontaneous and strong and honest. Honesty is very important. It's the backbone of a relationship."

Marc nodded his head.

She continued. "I want to make love at least three times a week and go on trips during vacation time and feel as though I can tell him anything. Most importantly I need a sensitive man."

Marc's eyes gleaned. "I can do that. I can be those things for you."

Katie was not so sure. She was 27 turning 28 in August and Marc had turned 23 in November. What was someone so young going to offer her? He had already told her that he was a student at McGill and was living in the ghetto with a friend. He was studying political science. Katie had just finished her master's degree at Concordia in media studies and was considering going back to do a PhD depending on how things went with the African show. She was making $70,000 a year and living in Montreal where her rent was $250.00. She had more than enough money and Marc was on an internship with "Dimanche Magazine" so he was not even getting paid.

He seemed ambitious though, even too ambitious and she wondered if he was looking for a free ride.

"Why are you interested in me?" Katie asked bluntly.

Marc did not miss a beat.

"You're beautiful. I like black women. I've liked them since I was 10."

"I'm not into being anyone's fetish."

"I don't see you as a fetish. I just prefer black women. I like you. You are beautiful. If you were white you would not be asking me that question. You would accept that I'm attracted to you. I prefer dark skin. I even prefer dark meat."

Katie had to smile. "I prefer white meat."

They had settled that.

"I have to wake up for work tomorrow," Katie said looking at 10:00 p.m. on her watch. "I also don't want to get home too late."

Marc shifted in his seat.

"I can walk you home. Where do you live?"

Katie lived in Notre-Dame-de-Grace (NDG), far from the Radio-Canada building. She had moved there while she was doing her graduate degree and did not move because the rent was cheap and it was a clean, small building. She had a three and a half which meant a one bedroom with a bathroom and a kitchen. Her tuxedo cat Enid was waiting to be fed.

"OK," she said. "I'm taking the Metro and you can meet my cat."

They took the Metro to NDG. Katie knew Marc was probably hoping to get lucky by bypassing the McGill ghetto where he lived and following her all the way to NDG. She decided she would sleep with him. She had even planned to make the first move.

Once they got into her apartment, she discovered how much Enid really liked Marc.

She was pleased by that. Enid was a good

judge of character.

After she fed Enid, Marc and Katie sat on the

couch. She planted a kiss on Marc's thin lips,

but discovered his tongue was where the

action was. They kissed for about 40 minutes

and then Marc abruptly stood up.

Katie looked up at him baffled.

"I know you have to go to work tomorrow, so we will continue this." He gave her a kiss on the mouth with tongue, the bulge in his pants obvious and left as quickly as he had entered her life.

Katie slowly rose from the couch and locked the door. She went back over to the couch and Enid came over to sit in her lap.

"Enid, what just happened?"

Katie was looking for an apartment the following weekend when she had time off. She had recently come from the hospital. Marc had been admitted to the psychiatric ward because he was not taking his medication. He was getting out that day and when he found out Katie was looking for an apartment, he wanted to come with her.

He came with Katie to see a four and a half, or two bedroom in an area called Villeray. Katie liked the apartment right away because it was minutes from the Metro. It was on the top floor of a triplex with two balconies and a fire escape in the back. The rooms were painted differently. The hallway was a golden yellow, the small bedroom she wanted to use as an office was brick red. The bedroom was a true blue and the living room was a peachy orange. The kitchen was in a leafy green.

Katie would have to buy a fridge and a stove. She was not worried because she was working and could afford that. The rent was $450 per month not including the utilities.

Marc liked it too. He lived in the McGill Ghetto with a roommate where he ended up spending a lot of time before he helped Katie choose her apartment.

Once Katie moved in, Marc was there all the time at first. After about two weeks they were having sex about three times a day. This was also around the time Katie lost her job. She received two weeks severance and went on unemployment insurance. Eventually she received work as an English as a Second Language Instructor.

Marc's internship ended and he planned to do a graduate certificate in international journalism through the University of Quebec in the city of Quebec. Marc is from a small town called Levis close to Quebec City. When the autumn came, he would spend the week in Quebec City and visit Katie every weekend.

Katie had been keeping a journal since she was seven-years-old. Marc gave her one in yellow that had pictures of bees on it and said "Bee Happy." She anointed her new prize, her new stable into her writing:

She will never grieve the loss of something old, because it means something new is happening.

Something different and dramatic is approaching on the horizon.

Katie would write: I would love to get the right to be a billionaire with a few trillion extra so I can go off on lavish vacations and the sort. I am getting a lot of good advice from those books. A lot of good summaries and quotations of the kind of things I'll be doing with my life. It will all fall into place -

and I'm not lazy. I'm not worried about a

thing. Marc knows I'm not the homemaker

type. There is just nothing I regret - and I am

not even having to turn back the hands of

time. Sweet justice to see me coming in there

- high and bothered. I don't know what

possessed me, but it was certainly something

that I needed to know before I proceeded to

the next level. I love myself, I love my

choices in life - it has all come down to milk,

purchased at a cheap price, available every

morning.

She would have received good recommendations and a salary raise if she had stayed freelancing at RCI. She felt like she was becoming more of an adult. She was happy when she was younger on her own in the world. She created. She liked school, sometimes, as long as they made it fun. Now she did not have to deal with peer pressure.

She was going to pick up that *Girl* magazine so could effectively ward it off. She was going to write a book, completed, published and marketable in a matter of a few days or weeks even. Live a life of adventure.

"Eyewitness News" had gotten to her long enough.

She wrote from her heat. She will take a spirit soul with her every time when she would say a prayer.

She was lying in bed with Marc while he was in town from his studies in Quebec City.

"It's interesting how much we take into our

system when tired," she said. "I am thankful to all the women and gay men who have struggled in the writing field making sure all of us brown folk will be able to write."

Marc nodded his head thinking of one of his favourite writers Gay Talese.

"Who gets published and who doesn't get published is a question. It is a question of who has voice, who doesn't. Who counts, who doesn't. At certain times I keep pinching myself that I'm not still sleeping. Will I be a proponent of welfare? The answer is trying to make a living from your guts and glory - from the thing that really makes me shake and sizzle."

"That's radio?" Katie asked him to make sure.

He nodded and kissed her.

Katie had a draft of the manuscript she was writing in bed with her:

"This profile reminds me of nothing in fact. I

think I'm trying to make too many breaks and pauses. I must find the peace of mind and serenity to do whatever I want, basing the consequences on a good outcome. Power to me pleases God!"

Marc paused.

"I'm thinking of depression," Marc said. "How I will be experiencing it in a new way it seems to be something that could happen again, as my doctor says. You tell me not to worry."

Then came the winter.

••

January 2001 to August 2001 - pre 911

Katie and Marc were hanging out in the

apartment when Marc told her he would be

going overseas for eight months. It was part

of his graduate program. He suggested they

break up during that time. Eight months is a

long time to wait for anyone. Katie's

suggestion was that if they were still meant

for each other, they would come together

once he was back. Neither of them really wanted that. They stayed together.

He left in January and Katie started a French immersion program at McGill University. At the same time she started her PhD at Concordia. Her loneliness drew her to eat.

She would have non-alcoholic Beck's beer and egg bread from Jean Talon Market. She would buy her éclairs from a bakery walking distance from her house. The loneliness also encouraged her to shop. She bought tons of second-hand CDs at a store called Cheap Thrills and bought some first-hand CDs at Archambault. All these things helped to fill the void.

When she felt just like being in the neighbourhood she would hang out at Dottie's place. It was a small coffee shop about five minutes walking distance from her apartment.

Dottie was a Jamaican woman who married a white doctor who had died. They had a daughter who was dating a handsome white boy at the time. Dottie didn't make good coffee, but Katie went to the coffee shop because she always had stories to tell. She would often talk behind the backs of the last customer that would leave. Katie would usually sit with two older guys, Joe and a retired doctor. Sometimes she would sit by herself and just talk with Dottie while she would be constantly sweeping.

Marc came back after three months to visit Katie. They had a wonderful time. By then she was still feeling as though they should not break up and she was willing to wait for him.

He had been to Paris and to Spain and would be leaving to go to South Africa to do an internship at the South African Broadcasting Corporation. He often spoke of his dream of the two of them living in South Africa.

After Marc left again, soon after Katie stopped doing the immersion program. She was not happy with her teacher and her fellow students. She was running out of money when her insurance benefits ended. School was also proving expensive.

A claimed psychic at Dottie's coffee shop told her that her father was going to commit suicide and that Marc only wanted her for sex. This scared Katie so much that she made plans to return to Toronto - her hometown.

When Marc emailed his psychiatrist that Katie would be returning to Toronto he wrote him a note to give to any new psychiatrist that he would have in Toronto to read. He said it would be difficult for him to move to Toronto.

He did not realize that Katie was not planning on him coming at first. He would probably have a hard time adjusting and he did not think things would go well.

Katie left for Toronto on April 8th, 2001. Her PhD research was done in Toronto.

Crush

I had a huge crush on this basketball player in high school. He also played hockey so I would dress up in little dresses and go with my bum warmer he signed for me into a cold arena and sit there and watch the games.

That night was a basketball game and I wore high heels that I had no practice at wearing to the event. I strutted around trying to get his attention and during a period break I was walking through a doorway and tripped over some guy's feet.

I must have been just about the height I am now which is about 5'10", and I fell like a tree onto a concrete floor.

I sprang up quickly, only realizing now how lucky I was to even be alive, and as my friends hovered around me while I was standing, I held my forehead where I was hit and felt a huge bump rising.

One of my friends was so grossed out, she said I had to go take a look at it.

I went to the bathroom, where if I wanted to get my crush's attention in a bad way, I had certainly found the way because he happened to see the bump on my head before I did.

I looked in the washroom mirror and was horrified at looking at myself – the elephant woman.

I had a huge bump on my head that when I looked up, I could see it. A teacher came to check on me and went to call my mother

My mother was shocked when she saw me and so scared. We went to the emergency room of a hospital nearby. I waited at least three hours in the emergency room, getting increasingly agitated and worried.

Finally a doctor saw me. He took x-rays and said there were just some burst blood vessels and to put ice on it, it would come down naturally.

I spent the next month walking around school with sunglasses on because as the blood vessels went down in my forehead, for some medical reason I have no understanding of, the blood was rushing to my eyes and they were constantly blood shot. Not to mention that I had short hair I usually slicked back and the bump was still there.

Needless to say, I got more love from my mother than from the crush. My forehead healed eventually as well.

For Years

I knew he was coming into my life before I even met him.

When I was in high school, I went to a restaurant on the Danforth of Toronto with some friends. One of my friends started reading the Turkish coffee leaves for me after our meal.

"A man with a baseball cap will come into your life," she said. "You will have a very long relationship."

I smiled. Being the type that was usually skeptical of these kinds of predictions...I thought nothing of it – until I saw him.

I graduated from high school and went on to university. While I was in my French class in second-year, I met him – Rudy.

I was sitting down with my friend who I worked in the library with. That friend looked a little like the singer Prince and everyone nicknamed him that. Rudy was wearing a St. Louis Cardinals baseball cap in red and grey. The first thing I noticed about him was his hat. The second thing I noticed was how tall he was.

I later came to discover that Rudy was hot property on campus. Many of the girls wanted to date him. I was already dating a very good-looking white guy named Will. I broke

up with Will to date Rudy – this is how it

happened:

At the end of the year, there was a Christmas

party for the French class. I was not doing

well in the class and really did not want to go.

I slipped into the campus pub a little late and

avoided sitting beside the professor.

Because I avoided sitting beside the

professor, I ended up sitting beside Rudy who

seemed eager to have me sit beside him. We

had an enchanted conversation the entire evening. He walked me home with his slick-heeled shoes coming close to falling on the ice on the canal in Ottawa.

Rudy lived in the other direction close to Mooney's Bay and I lived by some highrises at the end of the canal close to Carleton University. He came over to my place (keep in mind I was still dating Will).

My roommate Angela was home and all three of us had an interesting conversation. After

Rudy left to go home late into the night, Angela encouraged me to date him. It was obvious I preferred Rudy over Will.

Shortly afterwards, in the New Year, Rudy did ask me out for a date. I had already broken up with Will, who did not take it very well. He pushed me down on the bed and got aggressive with me. Oh well, at least it was done.

After our first official date, however really our second, Rudy and I dated for three years after that. We kept in touch for a long time and even though it's now late 2009, I actually spoke to him last year. I also crossed paths with Will who helped me to get a job on TV where I talked about when I fell down wearing heels in high school.

Filling Out Forms

There is something I want online. A question to some query about my book orders. Customer service can help. I need to fill out a form.

I am trying to apply to schools. I am trying to upgrade my credentials. It has been a long time since I have walked the line to graduation. I have to fill out forms.

I am trying to get some extra money from the bank. It is really my money I am trying to get. I need to fill out some forms.

Where does it end?

This constant filling out of forms.

God bless the scientists that are working on telepathic intelligence and remote viewing.

Thank you

Thank you to all of you who have taken the time to inspire me and help me create these stories. Most of all...thanks to the readers.

Donna Kakonge (BJ Carleton, MA Concordia)

is a freelance educator, writer and

broadcaster teaching journalism and

communications in Toronto, Canada. She's

also taught abroad. She received a Gemini

nomination for work done with the Discovery Channel. Please find out more information by using the Google search engine below.

Donna's _résumé_ is also available for potential clients.

You can purchase her e-books _what Happened to the Afro?_ , _How to Write Creative Non-fiction_, and _Spiderwoman_ at her _lulu.com_ storefront. My books are also available on Amazon's Kindle.

She's worked in every form of media, from print, radio, television and online with such places as *the Toronto Star, New Dreamhomes and Condominiums Magazine,* the CBC, BBC, Young People's Press, One80 Youth Media Group and Vision TV. Her work and travel have taken her to such places as Belgium, Germany, Spain, Uganda and South Africa.

Check out the recent stories and audio files for exciting free information.

To contact Donna Kakonge, you can email her at: dkakonge@sympatico.ca.

Also By Donna Kakonge:

What Happened to the Afro?

This graduate research paper is a case study that sheds light on the politics of black hair.

How to Write Creative Non-fiction

Writing is one of the hardest jobs in the world, and this book will give you the help you need to crack the market. Everything you wanted to know about the writing business and how to write, with exercises included.

Spiderwoman

This book of short stories crafted over many years and originally developed in a writing workshop at Carleton University includes the experiences of a young black woman in Canada, experiencing everything from travel to family tragedy and love.

My Roxanne

Written at the age of 17 and revised later in life, this novel is the story of Roxanne and Lance – an interracial couple who go through their ups and downs.

Being Healthy: Selected Works from the Internet

This book is a compilation of works from the Internet related to health that have been edited by Donna Kakonge.

Do Not Know

This book is a collection of literary explorations of madness. A young black woman experiences the challenges and adventures of mental illness.

My Story of Transportation

This book is a memoir of Donna Kakonge's transportation experiences. Everything from roller skates to Jaguars; this is a story of how she has managed to get around.

Draft: Spirituality Chats

On a desperate search for a PhD, Donna Kakonge actually produces doctorate-level work by discovering there is more knowledge in one's common sense than meets the third eye of psychics.

Journalism Stories Collection

From newspapers and magazines such as NuBeing International, Panache, Pride, Share and the Toronto Star – Donna Kakonge creates a collection of her journalistic stories that span five years of her writing career.

The Education Generation

Perfect for professors, students and anyone in the college or university system in North America, this book has articles and columns that explore the notion of the education generation.

Digital Journals and Numerology

This book is meant to emphasize how powerful keeping a journal can be with the aid of numerology. I started writing one at the age of seven and keeping a journal has been a constant for me – more than some friends, some jobs and some family members. I used to get a thrill selecting my journals to write in. Now I have decided to try something new by using the computer that I already spend so much time on and money on to show how powerful keeping any journal...even a digital journal can be. Using the principles of numerology can also help in chronicling your life.

Other Work:

"Nine"

This is a selection of some of Donna

Kakonge's radio documentaries done with the

Canadian Broadcasting Corporation, as well as

Radio Canada International.

"Matoke"

This audio book brings the story of Matoke from the book Spiderwoman to your ears.

"Church Sunday"

From the book Spiderwoman comes an audio story of the story "Church Sunday," first published in Concordia University's *Headlight Anthology* and reviewed by the *Montreal Gazette*.

In My Pocket

This book was written to help you during the perilous times we live in.

Morning English Lessons

This is a book that is ideal for helping you hone your English skills.

Where I Was

This is a memoir of Donna Kakonge's sometimes-difficult life spent in Montreal and her move to the place she grew up in, Toronto.

Draft: Part Two

What happens when you turn to psychics for answers? You discover God.

Radio and Television Announcing

This book gives some fundamental knowledge to radio and television announcing.

Ugandan Travelogue

Donna Kakonge goes back to one of her homelands to discover where home really is.

School Works

A collection of essays Donna Kakonge has done about the black press, black journalists and ethics in filmmaking through undergraduate work at Carleton University in Ottawa, Canada and graduate work at Concordia University in Montreal, Quebec.

Yes, School Works

A collection of communication essays done at the graduate level at Concordia University in Montreal, Canada.

School Works – Other Essays

This is a collection of undergraduate arts essays done at Carleton University in Ottawa, Canada.

Honest Psychic Chats

This conversation with psychics is the last

book in the series of psychic chat sessions

online.

The Write Heart

This is the last in a series of books about

journalism that started with How to Write

Creative Non-fiction and followed with Radio

and Television Announcing. This book deals with journalistic and non-fiction writing.

Story Ideas: Help For Writer's Block

This is a collection of unfinished stories that writers could pick up on to develop full-length stories.

Listening to Music

The experience of listening to Erykah Badu,

Sting and India.Arie.

This is How the Egyptians Fell

Further conversations with psychics lead to a deeper understanding of how bogus this business really is. This is why the Egyptians fell.

Natural Beauty

Tips, information and advice on all forms of being a natural beauty.

Random Bibliography of Media Books and Internet Resources

This is a resource guide for media professionals, as well as students. It is also available as a free download.

My Mind Book

This is a guide of how to manifest the law of attraction.

Stories in Red and Yellow

This is a collection of fiction and non-fiction work.

www.ingramcontent.com/pod-product-compliance
Lightning Source LLC
Chambersburg PA
CBHW031523040426
42445CB00009B/370